P9-CNF-405

Larry Burkett's
Consumer Books For Students

renting
your
first
apartment

Larry Burkett's
Consumer Books For Students

renting
your
first
apartment

Larry Burkett
with **Ed Strauss**

Illustrated by **Ken Save**

MOODY PRESS
CHICAGO

Text & Illustrations © 2000 BURKETT & KIDS, LLC

Larry Burkett's Money Matters For Kids
Executive Producer: *Allen Burkett*

For Lightwave Publishing
Managing Editor: *Elaine Osborne*
Project Assistant: *Ed Strauss*
Text Director: *Christie Bowler*
Art Director: *Terry van Roon*
Desktop Publisher: *Andrew Jaster*

All rights reserved. No part of this book may be reproduced in any form without permission in writing from the publisher, except in the case of brief quotations embodied in critical articles or reviews.

All Scripture quotations, unless indicated, are taken from the *HOLY BIBLE, NEW INTERNATIONAL VERSION®. NIV®.* Copyright ©1973, 1978, 1984 by International Bible Society. Used by permission of Zondervan Publishing House. All rights reserved.

ISBN: 0-8024-0981-4

1 3 5 7 9 10 8 6 4 2

Printed in the United States of America

table of
contents

how to use
this book

Shortly after leaving home, many teens and young adults embark on a learning curve so drastic that it resembles a roller-coaster ride. Things they never did before—such as operating a washing machine, paying bills, shopping for groceries, renting an apartment, using a credit card—suddenly become sink-or-swim survival skills. Most teens fail to learn these basics while still at home and are woefully unprepared for life in the real world when they move out on their own.

The four books in this series—*Getting Your First Credit Card*, *Buying Your First Car*, *Renting Your First Apartment*, and *Preparing For College*—were written to fill these gaps in modern education and to teach you the basic life skills you need to survive in today's jungle. In this series we walk you step-by-step through buying a used car without being conned, using a credit card without diving into debt, going to college without mortgaging your future away, and renting an apartment without headaches.

These books contain a wealth of commonsense tips. They also give sound advice from a godly, biblical perspective. It is our prayer that reading the books in this series will save you from having to learn these things in the school of hard knocks.

To get the most out of these books, you should photocopy and complete the checklists we've included. They're provided to help you take on these new tasks step-by-step and to make these books as practical as possible.

Each book contains a glossary to explain commonly used terms. If at any point while reading you need a clear definition of a certain word or term, you can look it up. Each book also contains a helpful index that allows you to find every page where a key word or subject is mentioned in the book.

do you need *to move* out

do you need to
move out?

leaVing tHe nesT

So, you'll be graduating soon and you're thinking of moving out. You stand poised on the edge of the nest, your downy little wings spread, about to hurl yourself into the bottomless void of the real world. *Wait!* There are some things you need to know before you leap. First of all, do you *need* to do this? And if so, is *now* the time?

If your parents want you to leave, or if you're going to a university in another city, ignore these questions. Or if you're about to get married, leaving home is usually inevitable. "For this reason a man *will* leave his father and mother" (Matthew 19:5, italics added).

wHat's thE big hUrrY?

But if *you're* the one gearing up to go and your main reason for leaving is to be out from under your parents' restrictions, there are a number of things to consider to keep you from a crash landing. Experience can be a good teacher, but it can be an expensive one. That's worth bearing in mind, especially since you'll be paying all the bills.

First of all, it's not wise to leave home unless you have a secure full-time job. Once you've made your declaration of independence and you're of legal age, it is not your parents' responsibility to bail you out in a pinch, give you rent money, buy you groceries, do your laundry, or give you your inheritance forty years early. And remember, you'll need to have *had* that job for several months *before* leaving home, because you're going to be hit by a number of hefty expenses about an hour after you walk out the door.

altErnatIves tO apArtMents

1. Paying rent at home. When they first leave home, most young people rent an apartment. But there are other alternatives. First, there's the time-honored practice of simply staying put for a while and paying room and board to your parents now that you have a job and can help out. They'll probably charge you a lot less than it would cost you on your own, so you may want to take advantage of this period of parental subsidy to put as much money into savings as you can. You'll need it.

In fact, if they see you're serious about saving up every penny you can toward the day you move out, they may not charge you anything. Talk it over with them and come to an agreement.

If you're itching to be independent, continuing to live at home may not seem like such a great option, but it is literally about the *best* option going. Why? Because, as the following chapters show, setting up, renting, and furnishing an apartment is expensive. This is especially true if you plan on buying a car around the same time. (See another book in this series, *Buying Your First Car.*)

Renting at home for another six months or a year while you build up your savings will allow you to live comfortably, without having to scrimp and barely get by—or worse yet, go into debt to finance your purchases. One of the biggest traps people fall into when leaving home is to get a credit card and charge it to the limit to buy the things they need. Result? More than 50 percent of American young people with credit cards are saddled with debt and paying exorbitant interest charges month after month. (See another book in this series, *Getting Your First Credit Card.*)

2. Room and board. An alternative to living at home is to room and board with another family. When you pay room and board, you get a bedroom to sleep in and keep your things in, one to three meals a day, plus use of the home's laundry facilities, etc. You're sort of like a paying guest. Usually, however, their rates will be significantly higher than your parents would charge. (Come to think of it, your old room doesn't look so bad after all!)

3. Buying a place. Buying your own home or apartment is probably not an option at this stage. If it is, great! Where did you get all the money?

4. Co-renting with friends. You may be planning to move into an apartment with a friend and split the rent, or move into a house with several friends and really divide the expenses. This can save a lot of money, and it's proven to be a workable solution for a lot of people. But it doesn't always work. Co-renting often comes with real problems and pitfalls. (We'll come to that in chapter 5.)

5. Student residence. If you're going to a college or university, all of the above options still apply. In fact, every semester, colleges may publish a list of places that offer room and board to students. In addition, however, you may want to consider living in a student residence. This will typically be a small room with only the bare essentials: a built-in desk, bed, and closets. There will usually be a shared bathroom down the hall. The room will probably not have a kitchen, since there will be a cafeteria nearby too.

You can save even more money by having a roommate, but be careful: You could end up with a bad companion, or someone you can't get along with.

6. Co-op student housing. With co-op student housing you have your own room within a building that has bedrooms plus common areas. It's even cheaper than a student residence, but requires you to do some work to lower your rent. For example, you might have to work in the building's cafeteria every second week, or do certain cleaning chores. Not a bad deal, really, if you're trying to save money.

are **you** read**y**?

Chapter Two

are you
ready?

spEndiNg eVery peNny

Many young people suffer stress and anxiety and go into debt within a year or two of being on their own because they never learned to budget or save money when they were still at home. For too many teens the motto is, "If I have money, I'll spend it." But they soon find out that "there is no free lunch in America." Neither is there free breakfast, dinner, rent, electricity, gas, phone, cable, utilities, or groceries. Most landlords insist that rent be paid on the first of every month, and won't understand that you used the money to buy a new stereo and sound system.

For many young people, what starts out as a happy leap to freedom ends up as a rough wake-up call in a financial emergency room. Most American teens who live at home have no concept of budgeting or saving. They spend their money on brand-name clothes, state-of-the-art stereos, and going out with friends. Suddenly 75 percent of their budget is no longer available for luxury. Now it's more like, would you believe, 10 to 15 percent?

leArniNg tO budGet

That is why it is vital to learn to manage a budget *before* you leave home. You must learn to live on what you will earn each month when you move out. Learning to budget is not simply good advice. It is an essential survival skill. Unrestrained spending habits will sink you just as surely as an iceberg took out the Titanic.

We've included a form on page 44 entitled "Monthly Income & Expenses" which we recommend you photocopy and use. In chapter 8, under the section "Outflow," we will prioritize the categories in this budget, but for now, here's a brief introduction.

grOss aNd neT

The government taxes your *gross* income—the full amount you earn. Taxes are taken off the top before you ever see your paycheck. Also removed is money toward your pension plan, medical plan, unemployment insurance, etc. What you have left when you cash your check is your *net* income. This net income is what you have to actually spend on bills from *Housing* to *Miscellaneous*. That's why this is called your *Net Spendable Income*.

You will notice that *Charitable Giving* is right at the top of the list. Whatever amount you give should be based on your gross income. If you tithe and your gross income is $1,000 a month, God gets $100 right off the top—not 10 percent of your income after taxes. "Honor the Lord with your wealth, with the *firstfruits* of all your crops" (Proverbs 3:9, italics added). Give to God first and He'll see to it that you have what you need (Matthew 6:31–33).

This is not license for you to spend foolishly and put nothing in savings saying, "God will take care of me." God expects His people to be diligent stewards over their money and to learn to budget "in order that they may provide for daily necessities" (Titus 3:14). So practice budgeting while you're still at home. Better to make your mistakes now while you're still cushioned from the consequences.

thE hArd, cOld facTs

The hard fact is that most American teens *regularly* run out of cash before the end of the month. They spend every penny they have and have nothing left. But in the real world, bills come due at the end of the month and failing to pay them is serious. Repeatedly paying your rent late is grounds for eviction. Failing to make timely payments is also grounds for having your car confiscated, your stereo reclaimed, and your phone cut off. So get into the habit of paying your bills on time. And you can only pay them on time if you budget the money beforehand; set it aside and don't touch it.

You truly are on your own and responsible to look after yourself.

saVings vErsuS creDit

It is essential that you build up your savings before you leave home. You will need to buy furniture (including a bed), dishes, and a hundred other things, plus have a reserve in case you lose your job and are temporarily out of work—which sometimes happens to the best of us.

The temptation will be to get a credit card, have your parents cosign so you can get a credit limit of $2,000, and then buy the bed and other needs on credit. Bad idea. Not only is cosigning unscriptural, but plunging into debt the day you leave home can be disastrous.

By the time you finish paying off the purchases you charged, plus the high interest fees, you may have paid *twice as much* for those items as you would have had you paid with cash up front! (For an in-depth analysis of this subject, see another book in this series, *Getting Your First Credit Card.*)

wHat "oN yOur owN" mEans

Remember, once you're on your own, your parents are not obliged to do your laundry, cook your meals, or pay your rent. Remember those cooking classes you weren't interested in? Guess who's doing your cooking now? And if the dials on a washing machine are as confusing to you as the combination of a Swiss safe, your dirty laundry is going to pile up and up and up . . .

So while you're still at home, learn how to use the washer and dryer, change a light bulb, clean the oven, plan a grocery budget, shop, and choose bargains. In fact, your mom might let you practice doing the family grocery shopping for a month. You'll definitely get some feedback and pointers if you do that!

Learn how to make independent decisions. When you're actually on your own, your parents won't be there as a safety net to catch you, so while you're still at home, tell your parents not to wake you up if you sleep in, not to remind you of job interviews or appointments, not to loan you money in a pinch, but to let you experience the consequences of your actions. Live as if you were already on your own. Then, when you actually move out, you'll be ready.

yoUr wAlk wiTh God

You also now have to take full responsibility for your walk with God, which includes time reading the Bible and time spent in prayer. Though it's fine to spend your weekends relaxing with friends, too many late Saturday nights will get you completely out of the habit of going to church on Sunday. No matter how faithful you are to set the alarm, you're not going to get out of bed if you're practically comatose.

Skills You'll Need
Before You Leave Home:

Before you leave home, make sure you have these skills. (Check them off the list as you conquer them.)

____ Know how to live on a budget.

____ Know how to save money for future expenses.

____ Know how to write checks.

____ Know how to balance a checkbook.

____ Know how to do laundry without mixing whites and colors.

____ Know how to cook several different meals.

____ Know how to pay bills, promptly and in full.

____ Know how to clean the oven, the fridge, and the bathroom.

____ Know how to clean sink drains and change light bulbs.

____ Know how to keep your room clean.

____ Know how to go grocery shopping and find bargains.

____ Know how to buy for household needs.

____ Know how to make doctor and dentist appointments.

____ Know how to manage a schedule.

can you **afford** it

Chapter Three

can you
afford it?

mOre thAn rEnt

You may be able to afford monthly rent for an apartment, but if that's *all* you can afford, you're going to be sitting on the floor without furniture, without lights, without heat, without a TV, and with the window open for the carrier pigeon because you have no phone. Clearly, you need to factor in a lot more than just rent.

renTal rAteS

Rents vary widely from one city to another and even from one end of the city to another, so compare prices—and not just between apartments. You can rent a studio apartment, a one- or two-bedroom apartment, a basement suite, a room in someone's home, a duplex, a townhouse, a housing cooperative, a house, etc. And of course, the month you leave home, you can only choose from what's for rent *that* month. If you're in too much of a hurry, you might end up moving into a real dump simply because it was the only available, affordable place at the time. So why not wait an extra month till something better comes up?

tOtal hoUsing cOsts

OK, a month has passed. Now there's a better selection out there. But which place do you rent? That depends on how much money you have available each month. How much is that? We suggest that you allot 30 percent of your *Net Spendable Income* for housing, but as you can see from the form on page 44, this includes more than just rent. It also includes phone, water, gas, electricity, sanitation, etc. So calculate what 30 percent of your money is, and then total the figures in the *Housing* category. Whatever's left over is what you should be spending on rent.

Besides calculating all the monthly expenses of living on your own, don't forget the one-time start-up costs. These are:

1. Security deposit. A security deposit is money that the landlord requires up front before you move in—on top of your first month's rent! In some states, this deposit is half a month's rent. In Missouri it can be as much as two month's rent. What is a security deposit? In a national survey, only 43 percent of high school seniors in America knew that this money was to cover the cost of damages (accidental or intentional) caused by the tenant. Presumably, Canadians would score slightly higher, since their name for this money is "damage deposit."

2. Phone connection fee. You do want a phone, don't you? Great! They're less messy than carrier pigeons. If you have the cash, the phone company will be happy to hook you up and give you a number. For a fee, naturally. Check what the rates are in your state and city.

3. Cable connection fee. OK, we didn't try to talk you out of getting a phone, but you should ask yourself: "Do I need cable?" Before you answer, *first* ask the cable company how much your hookup will cost. Add to that the monthly fees. *Now* ask yourself, "Do I need cable?" (Hint: You don't need cable in order to use a VCR and watch videos.)

4. Furniture and equipment. Obviously, you will need a bed. And a table and at least one chair, maybe a TV, and a lot of other things. Fridges and stoves usually come with the rental unit, and most apartment buildings have a coin washer and dryer you pay to use. See chapter 4 for a complete checklist of the furniture and equipment you will need.

5. Moving costs. Most people find friends who have pickups they can move furniture in, then thank them profusely, usewarming party, and invite their friends to it. ...ave so much furniture that you need a moving ...ly—you'd better phone a company and find out ...t costs to rent one for a day.

...ι we suggested that you put aside money in savings toward the day you move out. Now you see what those savings were for. Let's add them up and figure out exactly how much you need to save.

Start-up costs:

$_____	Security deposit	$_____	Phone connection fee
$_____	Moving costs	$_____	Cable connection fee
$_____	Household supplies	$_____	Furniture and equipment

And don't forget—

Rental rates for either (half, if co-renting):

$_____	Studio apartment	$_____	One-bedroom apartment
$_____	Two-bedroom apartment	$_____	House (all, or just one floor)
$_____	Townhouse	$_____	Basement suite
$_____	Duplex	$_____	Room and board

$_____ TOTAL COSTS

Ongoing costs

Besides rent, please take note of the many other monthly expenses that appear on the budget form on page 44. From now on, you are the one responsible to pay your electric bills if you don't want your power cut off. You are the one who needs to remember to pay your phone bill, keep milk in the fridge, and keep your medical plan current. How do you do this? Keep your bills in a safe place where they won't get lost, mark your calendar, and pay them on time.

planning
and
purchasing

We've decided to make our own furniture!

planning and
purchasing

saVing & bUdgEting

Once you know how much money you need to save in order
to move out, figure out what you can put into savings each
month, and from there, set a realistic date for moving out.
Then seriously start saving and discipline yourself to live
within a budget, so when it's time to move you'll be in pretty
good shape. Instead of being forced to rent a place with peel-
ing paint, sizzling electrical outlets, and curling linoleum,
you'll be able to afford a decent, modern apartment.

What about furniture? If you're paying room and
board in someone else's home or renting a furnished
apartment—or sometimes when renting a basement
suite—everything is supplied. About all you need to bring
is your own towels and bedding. But if you're renting anywhere else, most rental units won't have much more than
a stove and refrigerator, and you have to provide everything else.

Before you leave home, you'll also need to have the
financial wherewithal to meet the ongoing expenses and
bills on a monthly basis. This not only means getting a paycheck from a steady job, but disciplining yourself to divide
up that paycheck into the budget categories we give on the
form on page 44.

wHat dO yOu neEd?

At the end of this chapter is a list of basic things you'll need.
It's a good idea to start shopping around now for the smaller
items so you can get the best bargains and avoid a last-
minute rush. Check off these items as you purchase them.

You've probably noticed that we do not have "Huge Stereo" or "40-inch TV" on the list. Sorry. These are not priorities. If you want them when you move in, just delay leaving home a few more months while you save the money to buy them—with cash up front. Remember, avoid charging anything on your credit card that you can't pay off at the end of that month when your statement comes due.

buYing uSed

If you're willing to do without a new 40-inch TV or a 200-gallon aquarium, equipping your apartment doesn't have to be expensive. You don't need to buy everything new. You'll have enough expenses already that you might want to save a few bucks by buying secondhand household items. Some things you may even get free. Your bed, for example. Chances are your folks will give you the bed you've been sleeping on for the past ten years. After all, who else would want it now?

hyGieniC cOnceRns

Speaking of beds: If you can't take your own bed with you, do not buy a used bed. They come with serious hygienic concerns, not the least of which is dust mites. Dust mites often infest old pillows and mattresses and fill them with their feces, which in turn cause allergies and other illnesses. So save up your money and buy a new bed. (Or, if you get a frame and headboard for free, at least buy a new mattress.)

The same holds true for couches. It's not a bad idea to buy a used couch—especially considering the price of a new one!—but don't buy a *really* used couch, no matter how cheap it is. Thoroughly clean and vacuum each piece of furniture before bringing it into your house.

gaRage sAleS anD tHrift sTores

Your parents may also have an old set of dishes they can give you, a can opener, some kitchen knives, etc. And it's worth getting up early Saturday morning to cruise around the garage sales. After all, about 90 percent of what's sold at garage sales are household items, and they often go cheap. A new vacuum cleaner, for example, can be pretty costly. But you can pick up a used one in working order for fairly cheap.

For couches, tables and chairs, coffee tables, and dressers, check out your local thrift stores. If you still can't find what you're looking for, there are always "Buy & Sell" magazines or "For Sale" ads in the newspaper.

Furniture and Furnishings

Check these items off as you purchase them.

Bedroom:

____ bed	____ pillow	____ pillowcases
____ sheets	____ blankets	____ dresser
____ bedside lamp	____ bedside stand	____ night-light
____ mirror	____ desk	____ desk lamp
____ alarm clock	____ comforter	____ wastebasket

Kitchen:

____ plates	____ bowls	____ glasses
____ cups	____ mugs	____ forks
____ spoons	____ knives	____ ladle
____ whisk	____ cutting board	____ kitchen knives
____ frying pan	____ cooking pots	____ mixing bowl
____ measuring cups	____ spatula (flipper)	____ toaster
____ microwave oven	____ coffeemaker	____ kettle
____ can opener	____ dishcloth	____ dish towels
____ dish rack	____ dish soap	____ oven mitten
____ garbage can	____ salt and pepper shakers	
____ rug near sink	____ popcorn maker (optional)	

Dining Room:
- ____ table
- ____ tablecloths
- ____ chairs
- ____ hot pads

Food:
- ____ flour
- ____ pepper
- ____ tea
- ____ condiments
- ____ sugar
- ____ spices
- ____ herbal tea
- ____ staples
- ____ salt
- ____ coffee
- ____ ketchup
- ____ etc.

Cupboards:
- ____ broom
- ____ vacuum cleaner
- ____ dustpan
- ____ paper towels
- ____ mop

Living Room:
- ____ couch
- ____ curtains
- ____ TV and TV cabinet
- ____ rug
- ____ phone
- ____ cushions
- ____ television
- ____ bookshelf
- ____ lamps
- ____ answering machine
- ____ armchair
- ____ VCR
- ____ coffee table
- ____ stereo (optional)
- ____ CD player (optional)

Bathroom:
- ____ shower curtain
- ____ shampoo
- ____ washcloths
- ____ fingernail brush
- ____ first-aid kit
- ____ plunger
- ____ bathtub mat
- ____ bath towels
- ____ toothpaste
- ____ laundry basket
- ____ bathroom mats
- ____ weight scale
- ____ soap
- ____ hand towels
- ____ toilet paper
- ____ pain reliever
- ____ wastebasket
- ____ cleaning supplies

Supply Closet:
- ____ light bulbs
- ____ batteries
- ____ umbrella
- ____ multiheaded screwdriver
- ____ pliers
- ____ laundry soap
- ____ candles
- ____ flashlight
- ____ shoe polish
- ____ matches

Closet:

____ clothes hangers	____ suitcase	____ jewelry
____ iron	____ ironing board	box (optional)

Other:

____ paper	____ pens	____ pencils
____ scotch tape	____ ruler	____ calculator
____ notepads	____ doormat	____ pictures (for walls)
____ computer and printer (optional)		

sharing *with* friends

sharing with
friends

beNefIts oF co-rEntiNg

Co-renting can be lots of fun and can cut costs—like, would you believe—in half. It's a very appealing option. After all, maybe you can't even afford to move out on your own, but with someone else paying half the rent, utilities, and groceries, you can. And you get to live with a close friend, not your eight-year-old brother.

Plus, you can afford a bigger and probably nicer place if you co-rent. You can rent a two-bedroom apartment and split the rent in half. Or you can rent a house or one floor of a house instead of an apartment, and split the rent three or four ways. Plus you can stay up later with your rowdy friends with no irate neighbors banging on your ceiling or floor. What could be better? Maybe the question ought to be: "What might be wrong with this picture?" Because with all its benefits, co-renting comes with some built-in problems.

drAwbAcks oF cO-renTing

Co-renting can save a lot of money. Or maybe not. It doesn't matter if you live according to a responsible budget if your *friends* don't know how and blow their share of the rent money on new ski outfits. You'd better know their spending habits before you move in with them, because their ignorance of budgeting—or inability to do so—will affect you bigtime. And having to constantly hound them to chip in for groceries can put a terrific strain on your friendships, not to mention your wallet.

leGal iSsuEs

If you and a friend (or several friends) are considering co-renting an apartment, make sure that this is legally permitted. If the landlord isn't sure, check with the city's planning and zoning commission. Give the zoning staff the address of the apartment and ask how the building is zoned. You may find that no more than three unrelated persons can live in the building, which may come as a shock if you *plus* three friends were planning to move in together. Or maybe the "three-bedroom" apartment actually only has two legal bedrooms.

liFesTyle aNd habIts

What are your friends' lifestyles? Are they Christians? Will their lifestyles mesh with yours? What if they want to watch shows you wouldn't watch? Do you sit facing the wall with plugs in your ears to avoid taking it in? What if they want to fill the place with guests, but you want to study? What if they invite over seedy characters you would never have invited? What if you're fastidiously neat but they're tediously messy, or vice versa? What if you buy new furniture but they constantly scratch or scuff it? What if they snore or sleepwalk?

iF tHey moVe ouT

If you can't afford to leave home *unless* you co-rent, you probably shouldn't leave home. Because if for *any* reason your friends decide to move out—you have an argument, a nicer friend invites one of them to a nicer place, they join the Marines—you're left holding all the bills. Bills you can't afford to pay alone. And this happens.

Or what if your friends lose their jobs and it takes them two months to find new ones? What if they're in no *hurry* to find new jobs, and you're stuck with all the bills? "Fine," you say, "I'll kick them out." Right. These are your *friends*. You're going to think twice before you kick out your best friends. So for a while you pay all the bills and they promise to pay you later. But how long can this go on?

The financial situation may not become urgent if four or five friends are living in one house and one person moves out. You'll probably still be able to pay the rent. But it could make you so anxious to get an additional renter that you lower your standards and allow a questionable character to co-rent, and soon money and other items begin disappearing. *Then* what do you do?

wRittEn aGreEmenTs

No matter how close your friend is, you should have some clear understandings and you should have them in writing. You are co-renting. You are not inventing cooperative socialism. You are not pioneering utopian democracy. These things have been done. What you are doing is co-renting, and the less original your arrangement is, the more likely it is to succeed.

Writing was invented in Sumer some 6,000 years ago. Even then people realized that if you wanted to really nail things down, you had to get it in writing. So write it down. (See the sample Co-renters' Agreement form at the end of this chapter.)

cleArlY dEfinEd reSponSibiLities

Make it clear who's responsible for what, who does what chores such as cleaning, cooking, etc. You might want to make a schedule and rotate these duties. Set certain house rules such as: Clean up all the messes you make; do not leave dirty dishes laying around; counsel with the other person before making major purchases that affect rent-paying ability, etc.

Make sure that all expenses are shared equally. This means rent, utilities, cable, and phone. Each person should also be responsible to pay for any long-distance calls he or she makes. You should also decide whether you'll share grocery expenses or each person will buy his or her own.

Decide whose name the various bills will be in. After all, that person will be held responsible if the others don't pay. Decide who will actually pay the bills and collect the money to pay them. Agree that all money will be turned in on time and in full.

cOntiNgeNcy agReemEnt

Co-renting *can* be a great way to cut expenses while living with a good friend, but there are some very practical things to consider. Many major problems can be avoided by prayerfully considering the friend you plan on co-renting with and by having written agreements ahead of time. (It's also a good idea to write in a contingency clause in case things don't work out.) Such an agreement might read something like the following Co-renters Agreement.

Co-renters Agreement

Rent and Bills. We, the undersigned, are co-renting. The rent for the dwelling, as well as the telephone and all utilities, will be in

_____'s name, who will be responsible to gather the money from the other co-renter(s) and pay the rent and all utility bills every month. In return, all the undersigned agree to faithfully and punctually pay their share of all bills.

	Total	Share		Total	Share
Rent	$_____	$_____	Gas	$_____	$_____
Electricity	$_____	$_____	Water	$_____	$_____
Sanitation	$_____	$_____	Telephone	$_____	$_____
Food	$_____	$_____	Insurance	$_____	$_____
Maintenance	$_____	$_____	Other	$_____	$_____

Food. If food bills are shared, the undersigned promise to contribute their share. If everyone buys their own food, the other renter(s) agree to respect each other's food and not eat it.

Duties. Everyone agrees to faithfully do his/her part—whether shopping, cooking, cleaning, washing dishes, etc.—as spelled out on the attached schedule. *(Spell out and attach one.)*

House Rules. All renters will abide by the house rules agreed upon on the second attached page. This includes such things as noise levels, videos and movies watched, respect for personal property, use of the phone, protocol for inviting guests over, and tidiness. *(You'll need to discuss this, then write out your decisions and attach the page.)*

Moving Out. Should any person decide to move out, that person must give the main renter one month's notice. If he/she wishes to move out sooner, he/she must find another renter that is acceptable to the main renter and all other renters. If the main renter wishes to move out, he/she must either transfer the rental agreement and bills to the name of the remaining person(s), or give a month's notice of the closing of the apartment.

Whatever furniture anyone brought when he/she moved in remains his/hers. If some furniture was bought together, the other(s) must buy out the other person's share.

_____   _____

_____   _____

Signed this day ____/____/____ *(Make a copy for each person who signed.)*

finding,
checking,
negotiating

finding, checking,
negotiating

fiNdiNg a pLacE

Some practical tips about hunting for an apartment. Where do you start? A good place to look—but not necessarily the best—is the ads in the local newspaper. Also keep your eyes open for "For Rent" signs on apartment buildings. This is basic, right?

A lot of landlords, however, don't advertise in the paper when suites become available. They'd be inundated with calls from all kinds of unsavory characters they don't want in their building. When a suite is vacated, landlords often ask good tenants if they have friends who need to rent. Or existing tenants often ask their landlords, "If a suite ever opens up, would you let me know? I have a friend who wants to rent here."

So how do you know when an apartment is becoming available? Ask friends who're already renting. Or if you want to get into a certain building and people in your church rent there, ask them to put in a word for you with their landlord. If you have requests in at three or four build-ings, something is bound to turn up soon. Stay at home until something does.

Or maybe people in your church rent rooms, or a duplex, or the basement of their house. You can also check your local college housing lists.

thIngs tO cheCk ouT befOre yOu chEck iN

If a friend is getting you into a building, you should meet the landlord ahead of time. And while you're visiting your friend, have a look at the condition of the building and ask your friend lots of questions. (See the section—"Ask Current Renters"—for a sample of questions to ask.) Don't be afraid to ask the landlord lots of questions also. Then, when a suite is vacated and you can have a good look at it, ask more questions such as, "How old is this fridge? Does it leak? Do all the wall outlets work?"

If you've read an ad in the paper and call the landlord, you're still going to have to set up an appointment, look around, and ask questions. The difference in this case is that you're not the first in line and a few other people may be interested in the same apartment.

dOn't rUsh in

You may feel that when an apartment is up for rent, you have to grab it quickly, before someone else gets it. But *don't* be pressured into a hasty decision. If you rush in, you may later wish you could rush out. Remember, good landlords are choosy. They want tenants who don't cause trouble, and if they think you're honest and quiet they may want to rent to you and hold off other potential renters long enough for you to make up your mind.

reFerEnces

Landlords will want to know if you have a steady job and how much you earn each month. They want to be sure you can pay the rent. They will ask for references as well, particularly the name and phone number of your last landlord. If this is your first time renting, give your parents as a reference. They will definitely call your parents, because if they have to evict you, you'll probably end up back home. The pastor of your church would be a good reference as well. If the landlord has any doubts, you can be sure he'll call and ask about you. He may call the police for good measure and do a criminal check on you.

cHecKing ouT tHe laNdloRd

You can check out the landlord as well. For a modest fee, you can get a list of the number of calls to the police from that apartment building. If there are lots of calls, it may not be a building you want to move into. You can also call your local Consumer Protection Agency and ask if any complaints have been filed against the landlord.

bUildIng inSpeCtioN ofFice

In addition, you can visit your local building inspection office. Since inspection reports are public record, check out the records for the past five years for the address in question. Check when the inspector visited, the repairs the landlord was ordered to make, and how soon the repairs were finished.

asK cuRreNt rEnteRs

If you only check *one* resource, however, it should be current renters. If they give a poor report, rent elsewhere. Try to talk to at least two tenants. Explain that you're thinking of renting and ask questions such as:

- Does the landlord respond quickly when repair problems are reported?

- Has the landlord completed promised repairs?

- What happens if you pay the rent late?

- Are common areas (sidewalks, laundry rooms, halls) kept in good condition?

- Are there any major repair problems in the building, such as heating that doesn't work properly, faulty plumbing, leaky roofs, faulty electrical circuits, etc.?

- Are there pests such as cockroaches or mice?—Or African killer bees? (Just kidding on the last one.)

- Are there safety or noise problems in the building or neighborhood?

otHer conSidEratiOns

Other things to consider are location: Is it near the college or university you'll be attending? Is it near your workplace? Is it near a bus stop or public transportation, or close to a shopping center? Noise level is another factor: Are the neighbors quiet, or does lots of partying go on? Are there children nearby? Children are nice but noisy, which is something to bear in mind if you need quiet to study. Is there an elementary school across the street? Is a major long-term construction project beginning next door?

Size is important. Is it large enough to meet your needs? Windows and light: What do you need to function well and be happy? You might find a basement suite cheap, but it often has little light. Do you study better when you can see the sun or is too much sun a distraction? Is parking provided beneath the apartment, in a driveway, or do you have to park on the street?

wHat doEs reNt inCluDe?

And even though the monthly rent may *seem* reasonable, *is* it? Does it include things like utilities? Cable? Heat? Parking? Or are these extra? If so, your monthly housing expenses could be higher than you think. Find out from the landlord ahead of time exactly what is included in the rent and what is not. He's required by law to tell you.

damage lists ***and*** dotted lines

damage lists and
dotted lines

daMagE liSts

Before you move in, a landlord should give you an itemized Damage List to sign. It will inventory the crack in the sink, the gouge in the wall, and whatever else the landlord noticed. But you'd better double-check the list to make sure it includes *all* existing damage. Otherwise, when you move out, the landlord will assume *you* made those cigarette burns in the carpet and took your butcher knife to the kitchen counter, and he'll use your security deposit to make repairs. So before you sign a Damage List, write down any other damages on the list.

   If a landlord doesn't think of drawing up a Damage List, write up your own, make two copies, and both of you sign both copies. It may take you an hour, but save you $200. That's worth the trouble. When was the last time you earned $200 an hour?

chEckiNg foR dAmage

Places to check for damage are: walls for gouges, scrapes, or paint chips; sinks, mirrors, and tiles for cracks; walls and ceilings for mold or water damage; carpets for stains and cigarette burns; doorknobs and locks that are loose; stove burners that don't work; wall sockets that short out; fridges that are too hot or cold, etc.

paIntiNg anD rePairS

If walls need painting, landlords often paint them before you move in. But if they don't, now is the time to suggest painting. If you won't move in unless they paint, and they don't want to paint, work out an arrangement where they buy the paint and you do the painting for a reduction in your first month's rent. The same applies if the carpets are crying out for a thorough shampooing and cleaning.

Now is also the time to request that any other needed repairs be made, such as broken toilet seats, loose doorknobs, patio doors that won't lock properly, water damage to shower tiles, and faucets that leak. This is the time to ask that lethal lead blinds be replaced. And if you're newly married and have a child, ask if the walls have lead paint. If they do, the landlord must repaint or you don't move in. He may not want to—because all these things cost money—so if you're a handyman or have a friend who is, you can offer to repair these things for a reduction in your rent.

oTheR dEtaiLs

This is the time to have the landlord show you how the breaker switches work.

We mentioned a security deposit in chapter 3. Now is usually the time you'll pay it. And if there is an electronic door opener for the underground parking, you'll pay a small deposit for that at this time.

thE doTteD liNe

OK. Now you're sitting at the landlady's desk and she hands you the Rental Agreement to sign. It's a few pages long and looks technical, and she's going to lunch in half an hour. You're under pressure to trust her and sign it without reading it. *Don't.* It could contain provisions that are very much to your disadvantage or even illegal. So read it. And especially if it's a lease—not a month-by-month rental—you're crazy to sign it without reading it. A landlady shouldn't mind. She can do other paperwork while you read.

ofFiciAl rEntaL cOntrActs

It would be wise to download your state's or city's standard rental agreement off the Internet ahead of time—or get a copy from city hall—and read it carefully before going to see the landlord. This will not only give you practice reading rental agreements, but help you to spot illegal provisions in the one your landlord wants you to sign (in Canada, you can find standard contracts under the Canada Mortgage & Housing Corp, at *www.cmhc-schl.gc.ca*).

And no matter how well you know your prospective landlord, whether he's a friend or she's an aunt, get the rental agreement in writing. You may think that's too "businesslike" and prefer to simply shake hands on it, but verbal or casual agreements leave a lot of room for misunderstandings and broken friendships. A written agreement is a safeguard.

Once you have signed the rental agreement or lease, keep your copy in a safe place with your other valuable documents.

kEys

And don't forget your keys. The landlord will probably warn you as she gives you the keys: *"Don't lose them."* If you do, it may cost you a couple hundred dollars, because she'll have to replace the lock on the front door and copy a new key for every tenant in the building.

hoOkuPs

Before you move in, call the electric and gas companies and let them know when you'll need their services. Buy or rent a phone, get a phone number, and let the phone company know that you'll need to be hooked up. If you want cable, call them to come by and hook you up.

scrUbbiNg aNd clEanIng

It's also a good idea to enter your apartment shortly before you move in and clean it thoroughly. The landlord may or may not have done this, but if he didn't, then wash the walls, wipe the counters, scrub the cupboards inside and out with warm, soapy water and Lysol. It's a lot easier to scour out the grime before the cupboards are full.

moVing iN

When the big day arrives, check that the phone and cable are hooked up. You'll be needing the phone on a day like this.

There are also a couple things to guard against. First, according to Murphy's Law, there is a 93 percent chance that it will be raining. Second, remember how much your security deposit cost? Well, some of the worst damage inflicted on apartments happens on your first day as you lug heavy, oversized, sharp-edged furniture through cramped doorways and stagger with them down narrow halls. It may be worth the trouble of taping foam or cardboard to the edges of your furniture.

By the way, don't dismiss your biggest, strongest friends before they help you move all that heavy furniture into the right rooms.

hoUsewArMing parTy

And when all your furniture and household stuff is moved in? Treat your friends who worked so hard to help you move. It's party time! Grab some pizza and drinks and celebrate! Quietly. Just be careful not to overspend and deal your budget a deathblow.

Monthly Income & Expenses

Annual Income _____
Monthly Income _____

LESS
1. Charitable Giving
2. Tax _____

NET SPENDABLE INCOME _____

3. Housing (30%) _____
  Mortgage (Rent) _____
  Insurance _____
  Taxes _____
  Electricity _____
  Gas _____
  Water _____
  Sanitation _____
  Telephone _____
  Maintenance _____
  Other _____

4. Food (17%) _____

5. Auto(s) (15%) _____
  Payments _____
  Gas & Oil _____
  Insurance _____
  License _____
  Taxes _____
  Maint/Repair/
    Replacement _____

6. Insurance (5%) _____
  Life _____
  Medical _____
  Other _____

7. Debts (5%) _____
  Credit Cards _____
  Loans & Notes _____
  Other _____

8. Enter. / Recreation (7%) _____
  Eating Out _____
  Trips _____
  Baby-sitters _____
  Activities _____
  Vacation _____
  Other _____

9. Clothing (5%) _____

10. Savings (5%) _____

11. Medical Expenses (5%) _____
  Doctor _____
  Dental _____
  Drugs _____
  Other _____

12. Miscellaneous (6%) _____
  Toiletry, Cosmetics _____
  Beauty, Barber _____
  Laundry, Cleaning _____
  Allowances, Lunches _____
  Subscriptions, Gifts _____
    (Incl. Christmas)
  Special Education _____
  Cash _____
  Other _____

TOTAL EXPENSES _____

Net Spendable Income _____

Difference _____

upkeep ***and*** outflow

upkeep and *outflow*

uPkeEp

Once you're into your place, you need to think about upkeep. You launched a major cleaning campaign before moving in. Now you need to clean regularly. Here are a few other basic dos and don'ts:

- *Do* use the cutting board! Do not—I repeat, do *not*—hack up your counter while dicing carrots because you just can't bother to get the cutting board out of the cupboard.

- Remember how much grease there was on the stove and vents? Avoid grime buildup by always covering your frying pans.

- Regularly check your fridge and throw out moldy leftovers.

- Promptly tell landlords when anything breaks, fridges start leaking, toilets decide not to flush, heat vents won't work, etc.

- Clean up spills on the carpet immediately! If you don't know what cleanser takes out a certain kind of stain, phone Mom.

- Don't indiscriminately punch nail holes in the walls.

- If your friends still live at home, make sure they know your rules and respect your apartment and your neighbors when they come over. They also need to allow you space.

- Shop wisely, look for bargains, and eat well.

- Keep the noise level down, especially late at night.

- Do not let friends crash at your pad if it's against the landlord's rules.

oUtfLow: paY yoUr bIlls oN tiMe

If you're renting on your own, the bills are all yours. If you're co-renting with friends, everyone needs to chip in faithfully. Know your share and be sure to give it on time. You will only keep a good credit rating if you always pay your bills on time. Never allow yourself to get a month behind in paying bills.

bilL-paYing pRioRitIes

What do you do when payday comes? If you look back at the budget form we included, "Monthly Income & Expenses," you know how you need to divide your paycheck by category. You may question the need for some of these categories. For example, you may look at category 6: *Insurance* and ask, "What do I need insurance for? Why not use that 5 percent for new clothes?" Or you may ask, "What? Only 5 percent of my income for clothing? I'm used to spending 35 percent of my budget on new clothes!"

These categories were developed by Christian Financial Concepts and fine-tuned over the years, and while they're not carved in stone like the Ten Commandments, they are truly sound financial advice. They are tried, they are proven, and they actually work. Though the percentages may vary slightly in your personal budget, to completely disregard these guidelines is to do so at your own risk.

If you abide by these categories and faithfully allot your money to them, you will spare yourself a great deal of financial trouble. Sticking to a regular budget will ensure that you will have the money to pay the bills in each category on time and in full.

Nevertheless, emergencies do come up, and for this reason we have developed a list of bill-paying priorities.

Whether you get your paycheck once at the end of the month or twice a month, this is the order in which you should pay your bills. There are certain bills such as rent that must get paid on time and should never be late, and others, such as new clothes or entertainment that would not actually suffer if—due to unavoidable circumstances— you simply didn't have the money left over.

1. Giving to God. First, give to God. This shows that you acknowledge that everything in your life comes from God and belongs to God. As Psalm 24:1 says, "The earth is the Lord's, and everything in it, the world, and all who live in it." That *all* includes you and everything you own! If even you don't belong to yourself, but have been bought with a price (1 Corinthians 6:19–20), surely your money and possessions belong to God too.

When you give to the church, you may sometimes feel that you're sacrificing, but face it: It all belongs to God. Solomon, rich as he was, confessed, "Everything comes from you, and we have given you only what comes from your hand" (1 Chronicles 29:14). It would be good to settle on a specific amount that you give every Sunday. Many people choose to begin by giving 10 percent of their income to their church and other Christian ministries.

2. Paying your rent. After you have given to God, you must pay your rent. If you don't have enough money left to pay your electric bill, your power will get cut off, but at least you'll still have a place to live. On the other hand, it makes no sense to pay your electric bill but not be able to get into your apartment to enjoy the heat. The ideal, of course, is that you budget your money properly so—barring an emergency—you should be able to pay both.

3. Your other bills. Pay your regular bills. These include your electric bill; your gas, water, and phone bills; car payments; and debts (such as credit card payments if you have an outstanding balance). And if you have any other bills, such as cable or E-mail, now is the time to pay them.

4. Groceries. Buy groceries. Yes, food is fourth in line, not first. You may say, "But what if I don't have any money *left* for food?" Simple: Draw up a monthly budget and live by it. If you do, you'll always have 17 percent of your income available for food. The only reason you wouldn't would be if you made a major *un*budgeted expense—such as buying a new couch—and used your food money to pay for it.

The obvious solution is to never make *any* purchase that doesn't fit within your monthly budget. If you actually need something and your budget can't handle it, take the money from your savings account. "Savings?" you ask. "*What* savings?" Read on. All shall become clear.

5. Transportation. After you've set aside money for food, buy your monthly bus pass or put money aside for gas. You'll notice that 15 percent of your income is earmarked *Auto.* You've already made your car payments and paid your car insurance—and now you have gas and oil—so put the rest of the auto funds into an envelope marked "Maintenance & Repairs." Save this money for your regular tune-ups or for major repair work. It goes without saying that you should not "borrow" from this money to buy yourself a new set of skis. The same goes for the envelope marked "Insurance." Every month, put money toward next year's car insurance.

If you don't have an auto, then, after taking your transportation money out, put your entire auto budget into a separate savings account for a car. You eventually will need a car, and if you can pay in cash you'll save thousands of dollars in financing charges.

6. Medical Expenses. At this point, put 5 percent of your income into an envelope marked "Medical Expenses" and don't use this money for any other purpose. Then, when you need to fill a prescription or have a tooth filled, you'll have the money for it.

7. Savings. You're probably still wondering where you're going to get the money to buy that couch. Well, here it is! If you faithfully put 5 percent of your budget into a savings account, you'll be able to buy what you need with cash, not credit.

8. Save up for a house. You're not going to want to live in an apartment forever. One day you'll not only want a house, but you'll probably need one. You may not be able to set aside a whole lot toward a house in the beginning, but if you make a habit of it and faithfully put something toward it in a savings account every month, it will slowly build up. One day it will be enough to make the down payment.

9. Clothing. Need new clothes? Now's the time to buy them. You will notice, however, that this section is not titled New Clothing, only Clothing, which means that you are perfectly free to save money and buy some classy, new-looking duds at your local thrift store.

10. Entertainment/recreation. If you have any money left, use it for whatever you want. Go to a movie, have a short vacation, enjoy some ice cream. "*What* money left?" you ask. Well, according to the budget, you should have 7 percent of your income left for these purposes. If not, you're spending it somewhere else.

things you really *should* know

things you really
should know

baSic rIghTs oF all tEnAnts

Whether you're renting in Gator Bayou, Louisiana, or
Stampede, Montana, or downtown Los Angeles, all tenants in
America have certain basic rights. They are:

- The right to a livable dwelling. (e.g.—If your circuit breaker burns out, the landlord must restore your electricity. If
he wants you to leave, he cannot turn off your gas.)

- Protection from unlawful discrimination. (e.g.—A landlord cannot harass you or evict you because of your
race, ethnic origins, or religious beliefs.)

- The right to hold the landlord liable for damage caused
by the landlord's negligence. (If he failed to repair the
toilet and it overflowed, flooding your apartment, he
must pay damages.)

- Protection against lockouts and seizure of personal
property by the landlord. (She can't lock you out of
your dwelling, then sell your TV and your wardrobe.)

To find out what other rights you have, download a
copy of your state's *Landlord-Tenant Act* from the Internet or
go to city hall for a printed copy. Or phone and ask that it
be mailed to you. If you live in a large urban center, get a
copy of your city's laws as well, since they may have additional provisions. A landlord is not allowed to enter a rental
unit without proper advance notice, but what is "proper
notice" in *your* state? One week? Five minutes? Find out.

rEntiNg, a leGal agReemEnt

Some pages back, we told you not to sign a rental agreement

that contained illegal provisions. Each state—and often individual cities—have their own landlord-tenant laws, but regardless of the state, all tenants in America have certain basic rights.

If, for example, you signed a contract that didn't require the landlord to pay for repairs needed to make the dwelling habitable, that would be an illegal provision and would not be binding *anywhere* in the United States, particularly in Alaska in the middle of winter.

However, the landlord could write in provisions that are not illegal, but could make life difficult for you. For example, he could require that rent must be paid on the 28th of every month. That's before you get *paid*, right? So remember, renting is a legal agreement. And leasing is a *very* legal agreement! Once you sign the papers, you can and will be held liable to uphold your end of the bargain.

Before signing, negotiate with him. Go over the contract, point out any offending clauses, and explain why you would like him to change them. If he agrees, cross out those particular lines, write in a correction, and both of you initial each correction.

leAses vErsuS mOnth-tO-moNth rEntaLs

In an ordinary rental agreement you pay your rent month by month and can leave anytime so long as you give the landlord one month's notice. A lease, however, is an agreement to rent a dwelling for a specified time, often six months or a year. Let's say you signed a one-year lease for $300 a month, but after three months an emergency comes up and you have to move, or you get a job in another town.

Guess what! You can't just give a month's notice and leave. You have to stay the remaining nine months. Technically, you don't have to *live* in the house, but you *must* still pay nine months rent. In a high school competency test, only 40 percent of American teens knew this fatal little fact. Yet in this case, the answer is worth $1,800!

Most states do allow the lease to be broken *if* you find someone acceptable to the landlord to move in and take over your lease. But ever try that on short notice? Not easy.

rAisiNg thE rEnt

In the King James Version, Matthew 9:16 reads, "and the rent is made worse." Which goes to show—or maybe not—that it's no fun when your rent is raised. If you lease (say for one year), then the agreement will state that the rent cannot be raised until after the lease expires. On a month-to-month rental, a landlord must generally give a one-month notice if he's going to increase the rent. You may then opt to vacate if the increase is too big for your budget. How *much* can he raise your rent? If you don't live in a rent-controlled area, you can only hope he'll be reasonable. Often landlords are allowed to raise the rent "by any amount desired."

mAkiNg rEpaIrs

When something in their rental unit needs to be repaired, most tenants simply phone the landlady and mention it to her. You can do that, but the *required* legal procedure is for you to give her written notice. (And if your landlady has a habit of procrastinating, this is definitely the route to go.) The notice should include the date, address, and apartment number, the name of the owner, and a description of the problem. Deliver the notice personally or by certified mail.

You must then wait the required time for the landlord to begin making repairs. Depending on the state, this will be about twenty-four hours for no hot or cold water, heat, or electricity, or any life-threatening hazard; seventy-two hours for repair of refrigerator, range and oven, or a major plumbing fixture; ten days for all other repairs. Know your state's required waiting times before you set your stopwatch.

Even though you've discussed making the repair, the landlord or repair person can't just barge in and start work. She must give you proper advance notice. If she *doesn't* come or send someone within the specified period you can, if you wish, give written notice, move out immediately, and get your money back. A better option is simply to have a qualified repair person do the work and then deduct the cost from your rent. This is perfectly legal, but you must shop around for the lowest estimate and submit the estimate to your landlord before making repairs.

thE laNdlOrd's reSponsIbiliTies

Apart from fixing things that need repairs, what else is your landlord obliged to do? He must comply with housing codes; make repairs to the property; keep hallways, entryways, and so on safe and clean; keep the building safe and in working order; provide garbage containers and garbage removal; and place a smoke detector in each apartment.

He may or may not be responsible for other things. For example, who deals with the situation if your neighbors constantly party till 3:00 in the morning?—and you've been angrily rebuffed or icily ignored every time you knocked on their door and requested they be quiet? Many landlords will have no qualms about dealing directly with the tenant. Others will insist that it's *your* responsibility to call the police.

Apart from his responsibilities, the landlord has certain *rights* such as the right to collect rent on time, the right to spend your security deposit to repair your damage, and the right to evict you if you don't fulfill your responsibilities. Which brings us to the next section. . . .

thE teNanT's resPonsIbilitIes

Keeping these simple guidelines will save you from being evicted.

- You are required by law to pay your rent. Furthermore, you are required to pay it on *time*. If you're a couple days late paying rent—and this isn't the first time—the landlord can legally evict you.

- You must not disturb the other tenants. Keep the volume on your TV and stereo down, and no late parties when people on the other side of the paper-thin walls are trying to sleep. If the building has a noise curfew at 10:00 or 11:00, *keep* it.

- You must keep your apartment safe and clean and remove your garbage regularly.

- If the contract specifies "no pets," that's what it means. Don't try to sneak in your cat and claim, "But he's family!"

aVoiD bEing eVicTed

Don't kid yourself by thinking, *Oh, well, if this landlord kicks me out, I'll just move to a better building.* Your renting history creates a paper trail that can haunt you. When you're applying to rent a new apartment, they'll want the phone number of your last landlord. And if he says he had to throw you out, or even if all he says is that you were messy or late in paying rent, the new landlord could well refuse you. And he doesn't even have to give you a reason why.

Don't think, *I'll butter up my old landlord before I leave and ask him to put in a good word for me. After all, he wants to get rid of me.* Smart landlords make a point of calling your former neighbors as well to get the real lowdown on you.

Of course, "even though we speak like this, dear friends, we are confident of better things in your case" (Hebrews 6:9). We trust that you will be responsible, good tenants, quiet, considerate, and loving. Nevertheless, it sometimes helps to know where the boundaries of acceptable behavior are drawn, and the consequences of overstepping them.

moving ***out***
and on

moving out
and on

giVinG nOticE

Now you're moving out. Hopefully not because you're being evicted or because a tornado ripped the roof off the building. Maybe you just need a bigger and better place. So what should you do?

The first thing to do is to give notice to the landlord. How many days notice? Check your contract, but usually a tenant is required to give a landlord one month's notice. If you plan to move out June 30, you'll need to give notice *before* June 1.

If you're breaking a lease and don't want to pay several months rent, give written notice of your intent to vacate as early as possible so the landlord can find a new tenant quickly. In fact, it's in your own interests to *help* him find a new tenant to replace you. The landlord may not reasonably refuse to rent to someone else just because he wants to make life difficult for you.

cLeaNing ouT aNd clEaniNg uP

Move your furniture out carefully so you don't ding or scratch the walls. You don't want to lose your entire security deposit during the last half hour of your stay there, by damaging the apartment as you move out.

Be sure to thoroughly clean up after your furniture is out. Perhaps you're not legally required to clean the greasy wall near the stove or scrub the smudges off the hallways, but if you made the mess, clean it up. It's just plain love and consideration and part of your witness as a Christian. By showing the landlady you respect her apartment, you're showing that you value and respect her as a person.

getTinG yoUr sEcurIty dEpoSit bAck

If you've taken good care of the rental unit, you should get your full deposit back. A landlord cannot make you pay for ordinary wear and tear, but he does have a right to make you pay for cleaning a filthy carpet or repairing actual damage. If you caused any damage, honestly disclose it to the landlord. Don't hope he won't notice it.

A landlord may give your security deposit back the day you move out, but most often you'll wait a couple weeks or a month to receive it in the mail. If he doesn't return it and falsely accuses you of causing damage just so he can keep your money, take your copy of the damage list to show him. If he still refuses, you can sue him for the amount of the security deposit, sometimes twice the amount. You may choose to let yourself be cheated and defrauded (1 Corinthians 6:7) but the law is on your side.

soMe LEgaL isSueS

Abandonment is when a tenant abandons a rental unit. The landlord drives up to find no one there and the shutters flapping in the breeze. What can he do? Individual state's laws vary, but some states require him to wait a specified time before auctioning off any belongings the tenant left behind. And of course, he gets to keep the security deposit. (About the only legitimate reason a Christian would have for abandonment is if they were caught up in the Rapture.)

A *lockout* is when the landlord wants to get rid of you, so he locks you out. You go out for a jug of milk and come back to find the locks changed and all your belongings inside. The landlord may think he's within his rights, but he's way out of line. While you shouldn't attempt to kick the door in, you can and should take immediate legal action.

If the owner sells the building or apartment, he is required by law to inform you of the fact, and to give you the name and address of the new owner.

gEttiNg mOre inFo

If you have further questions or complaints, check with city hall or phone the numbers given on your state's *Landlord-Tenant Act*. If you have been unable to find a copy of your state's *Landlord-Tenant Act* on the Internet—and this is very possible, since each state lists these things differently—phone city hall and ask them to mail you a copy. At the same time, ask them for an Internet address where you can do further research.

If you have any complaints to lodge, ask for specific phone numbers you can call. They should also be able to refer you to Housing Mediation Services, should you need them.

Disclaimer

No part of this booklet should be regarded as legal advice or considered a replacement of landlords' or tenants' responsibility to be familiar with their local and state laws. If you need legal assistance, contact a housing attorney, a Housing Mediation Service, or file a complaint with the number supplied in your state's *Landlord-Tenant Act*.

Glossary

Budget: A written plan where you allot a percentage of your income to pay each of your expense categories.

Co-renting: Renting a place (and sharing room and expenses) with one or more people.

Damage list: An inventory (list) of all existing damage before you move into a dwelling.

Eviction: When the landlord (either legally or illegally) forces you to leave your dwelling.

Illegal provisions: Conditions which uninformed landlords write into a contract, but which are neither legal nor binding.

Landlord-Tenant Act: A set of state laws which spell out the rights and responsibilities of both landlords and tenants.

Lease: An agreement to rent a dwelling for a specified time, often six months or a year.

Net spendable income: The net (remaining) income you can use to pay your bills after you have given to God and paid your taxes.

Proper notice: Before a landlord is allowed to enter your dwelling, he must notify you of his intentions several hours or days in advance.

Rental contract: A written list of conditions which you and a landlord agree upon and sign.

Rental unit: Any apartment, room, or dwelling which you pay rent to live in.

Security deposit: Money you give to a landlord before you move in, which he may then use to repair damage you cause.

Tenant: This is you, and anyone else who rents a dwelling.

Zoning: Laws which determine what property or dwelling can be used for what purposes.

Index

Larry Burkett's **Money Matters for Kids**™ is providing practical tips and tools children need to understand the biblical principles of stewardship. **Money Matters for Kids**™ is committed to the next generation and is grounded in God's Word and living His principles. Its goal is *"Teaching Kids to Manage God's Gifts."*

Money Matters for Kids™ and **Money Matters for Teens**™ materials are adapted by **Lightwave Publishing**™ from the works of best-selling author on business and personal finances, **Larry Burkett.** Larry is the founder and president of **Christian Financial Concepts**™, author of more than 50 books and hosts a radio program "Money Matters" aired on more than 1,100 outlets worldwide. **Money Matters for Kids**™ has an entertaining and educational website for children, teens, and college students, along with a special **Financial Parenting**™ resource section for adults.

Visit **Money Matters for Kids** website at: **www.mmforkids.org**

building Christian faith in families

Lightwave Publishing is a recognized leader in developing quality resources that encourage, assist, and equip parents to build Christian faith in their families.

Lightwave Publishing also has a fun kids' website and an internet-based newsletter called *Tips & Tools for Spiritual Parenting.* This newsletter helps parents with issues such as answering their children's questions, helping make church more exciting, teaching children how to pray, and much more.

For more information, visit Lightwave's website: **www.lightwavepublishing.com**

MOODY
The Name You Can Trust®
A MINISTRY OF MOODY BIBLE INSTITUTE

Moody Press, a ministry of Moody Bible Institute, is designed for education, evangelization, and edification.

If we may assist you in knowing more about Christ and the Christian life, please write us without obligation:

Moody Press, c/o MLM Chicago, Illinois 60610
Or visit us at Moody's website:
www.moodypress.org